Lives   ᴀᴵᴺᵀˢ

Our Lady of Lourdes

with Prayers and Devotions

Edited by
Mark Etling

Regina
Press

Nihil Obstat: Reverend Robert O. Morrissey, J.C.D.
                     Censor librorum
                     November 18, 2004

Imprimatur: Most Reverend William Murphy
                     Bishop of Rockville Centre
                     November 21, 2004

THE REGINA PRESS
10 Hub Drive
Melville, New York 11747

Printed in U.S.A.

ISBN : 0-88271-762-6

Introduction

Year after year hundreds of thousands of pilgrims gather at the Sacred Grotto of Lourdes in southern France. Most come for healing - healing of body, mind and spirit. Some come for healing for themselves, others to pray for healing for a loved one.

Many receive the healing they pray for. There are countless stories about pilgrims who come away from Lourdes free of the disease or infirmity that afflicted them. They believe they have experienced the healing mercy of God.

But others do not obtain the healing they seek. The cancer does not subside, the depression does not abate, the broken relationship is not mended. As believers, what are they - and we - to make of this?

The fact that not everyone receives the healing they seek at Lourdes testifies to the reality that Lourdes is a haven of faith, not magic. Just as there is not absolute certainty about the apparitions to Bernadette, so there is no guarantee that those who journey to Lourdes or who pray to Our Lady of Lourdes will receive the healing they seek.

This points to a crucial element of the Christian faith – that we are called to believe, above all, in the mystery of God's will for us and for our loved ones. Bernadette Soubirous responded in faith to God's will for her, even though her commitment brought with it much suffering. The story of Bernadette, and the lesson of Lourdes, is that we must always seek, and then accept, the will of God in our lives. Our greatest and most profound experience of healing comes, not in receiving the cure which we seek, but in submitting ourselves to the will of God – "Lord, not my will, but thine be done."

The Story of Bernadette and Our Lady of Lourdes

*T*he pages of Christian history are filled with the stories of otherwise little-known people whose lives are touched by God in profound ways. While the world is forever preoccupied with the lives of the rich and famous and powerful, God routinely seeks out the "little people" of this world to reveal his loving mercy to us. Such is the story of Bernadette Soubirous and Our Lady of Lourdes.

Bernadette was born in the French town of Lourdes on January 7, 1844, the oldest of nine children born to Francois and Louise Soubirous. When she was a small child her family experienced relative prosperity, and there was peace and harmony in the Soubrious family. This stability provided Bernadette with the strong emotional and spiritual foundation she would need later in life.

By the time young Bernadette reached the age of ten, however, hard times befell southern France, and a series of misfortunes touched the Soubirous family. A two-year drought struck the region, and this greatly diminished the wheat harvest. Eventually this caused Francois' mill to be put out of business, and he was out of work.

As a result the family was forced to move to a dwelling called the Cachot, which had just one room and had previously been used as a jail. Not long after this young Bernadette contracted cholera, which not only prevented her from attending school, but affected her health for the rest of her life. The family also suffered the indignities and insults of many in Lourdes, because they were reduced to living in poverty.

Because her poor health so often kept her out of school, by age 14 Bernadette could not read or write French, and could speak only the local dialect. She attended Mass, but made her first Communion later than the other children her age.

But on February 11, 1858 Bernadette Soubirous' life changed forever. After dinner that day Bernadette went out to the Gave river with her younger sister Marie and another friend to gather firewood. While searching for wood Bernadette heard a loud noise like the sound of a storm coming from a nearby hollow in the rock known as Massabielle. Then she saw a vision of a beautiful young woman above a rosebush which moved as though the weather were windy. Bernadette described the lady as clothed in white, with a blue ribbon sash and a rosary hanging from her right arm. The woman smiled at Bernadette and motioned for her to advance. Bernadette, without fear, fell to her knees to pray the rosary. After a time the woman in the apparition slowly withdrew to the interior of the hollowed out rock and disappeared.

Bernadette tried to keep the apparition a secret, telling only her sister what had happened. But soon the secret came out, and her mother Louise forbade Bernadette to return to Massabielle. Still, the vision would not leave Bernadette's mind and heart, and before long her mother allowed her to return.

During an apparition on February 18, Bernadette reported that the Lady said to her, "I do not promise to make you happy in this world, but in the next." These words would serve as a prophecy about the suffering that would mark the remainder of Bernadette's life.

After the fifth apparition on February 20, Bernadette said the Lady told her to always bring a blessed candle with her to the site. Bernadette heeded the Lady's directive and, as a result, the custom of burning candles at the Shrine of Lourdes continues to this day.

As time went on more and more family members, neighbors and villagers witnessed the apparitions, although only Bernadette was able to see the Lady. Eventually hundreds and even thousands of people would be present at the apparitions.

During the ninth apparition on February 25 the Lady told Bernadette to "drink from the fountain and bathe in it." This confused Bernadette, because at the time there was no water at the site. But Bernadette scratched at the ground, and soon a spring bubbled up. She cupped her hands together and drank the water, and then washed her face. Within two days the little pool had become a flowing stream. Bernadette reported that the Lady promised the spring would bring healing to those who came to use its waters.

On February 28, during the eleventh apparition, the Lady directed Bernadette to tell the local priests that she wanted a chapel to be built at the site, and that there should be processions to the grotto. At first the priests were skeptical of Bernadette's claim, and said they wouldn't believe her. Their skepticism would turn out to be short-lived.

By the time of the fifteenth apparition on March 4, almost all of France had heard about Bernadette and the beautiful Lady. No less than 20,000 people were present that day, including an entire military garrison in full dress uniform.

The sixteenth apparition took place on March 25, the feast of the Annunciation. On that day the Beautiful Lady finally revealed her identity to Bernadette, in these words: "Que soy era Immaculado Conception," which means "I am the Immaculate Conception." Bernadette herself did not know what this name meant, but the many who flocked in even greater numbers to Lourdes certainly did.

The eighteenth and final apparition occurred on July 16, even after the local prefect had ordered the grotto closed. Because the barricade ordered by the prefect was still in place, Bernadette and her aunt knelt in the grass to pray. On this day, the Beautiful Lady appeared to Bernadette for the last time.

In 1862, four years after the last of the visions, the bishop of the diocese declared that those who believed what had happened to Bernadette were "justified in believing the reality of the apparition." Soon thereafter a basilica was built upon the site by Fr. Peyramale, the parish priest.

At the age of 22, Bernadette entered the Congregation of the Sisters of Nevers. Although she continually suffered poor health, she was faithful in performing her duties as infirmarian and sacristan. She died at the convent of Nevers on April 16, 1879 at the age of 35.

In 1873, national pilgrimages involving people from all over France were started. Three years later the basilica was completed and consecrated, and the statue of Our Lady of Lourdes was crowned.

The foundation stone of a new church was laid in 1883, because the first church was no longer large enough for the crowds who were starting to come to Lourdes. This church was completed in 1901 and called the Church of the Rosary.

In 1907, Pope Pius X extended the observance of the feast of Our Lady of Lourdes to the whole Church, to be observed on February 11. Today people from all over the world come to pray and seek God's healing at the Sacred Grotto of Lourdes. Saint Bernadette was canonized on December 8, 1933.

Prayers to Our Lady of Lourdes

Novena to Our Lady of Lourdes

Opening Prayer: Be blessed, O most pure Virgin, for having appeared in the Grotto of Lourdes, saying to the child, St. Bernadette: "I am the Immaculate Conception." We marvel at your Immaculate Conception. And now, ever Immaculate Virgin, Mother of mercy, Health of the sick, Refuge of sinners, Comforter of the afflicted, you know our wants, our needs, our troubles and our sufferings. We ask you to look upon us with mercy.

By appearing in the Grotto of Lourdes, you were pleased to make it a privileged sanctuary, a place where many have obtained the cure of their infirmities, both spiritual and physical. We come, therefore, with complete confidence to ask your motherly intercession. Obtain for us, O loving Mother, the granting of our request. In gratitude for all your favors, we will endeavor to imitate your virtues, that we may one day share your glory.

Our Lady of Lourdes, Mother of Christ, you had influence with your divine Son while upon earth. You have the same influence now in heaven. Pray for us; obtain for us from your divine Son our special requests, if it be his holy will. Amen.

Our Lady of Lourdes, pray for us.
St. Bernadette, pray for us.

Day One

O Mary Immaculate, Our Lady of Lourdes, virgin and mother, queen of heaven, chosen from all eternity to be the mother of the eternal Word and preserved from original sin, we kneel before you as did Bernadette at Lourdes and pray with childlike trust in you that, as we contemplate your glorious appearance at Lourdes, you will look with mercy on our petition and obtain for us a favorable answer to the request for which we are making this novena (*mention your request here*).

O brilliant star of purity, Mary Immaculate, Our Lady of Lourdes, glorious in your assumption, triumphant in your coronation, show us the mercy of the Mother of God, Virgin Mary, Queen and Mother, be our comfort, hope, strength, and consolation. Amen.

Our Lady of Lourdes, pray for us.
St. Bernadette, pray for us.

Day Two

*B*e blessed, O most pure Virgin, for manifesting yourself with light and beauty in the Grotto of Lourdes, saying to the child St. Bernadette: "I am the Immaculate Conception." O Mary Immaculate, inflame our hearts with a ray of the burning love of your pure heart. Let our hearts be consumed with love for Jesus and for you, so that we may enjoy your glorious eternity. O Mary, take into your keeping and present to your divine Son the petition for which we are making this novena (*mention your request here*).

O brilliant star of purity, Mary Immaculate, Our Lady of Lourdes, glorious in your assumption, triumphant in your coronation, show us the mercy of the Mother of God, Virgin Mary, Queen and Mother, be our comfort, hope, strength and consolation. Amen.

Our Lady of Lourdes, pray for us.
St. Bernadette, pray for us.

Day Three

You are all fair, O Mary, and there is in you no stain of original sin. O Mary, conceived without sin, pray for us who have recourse to you. O star of holiness, as on that day upon a rough rock in Lourdes you spoke to the child Bernadette and a fountain broke from the earth, miracles happened, and the great shrine of Lourdes began, so now we ask you to hear our fervent prayer and grant the petition we so earnestly seek (*mention your request here*).

O brilliant star of purity, Mary Immaculate, Our Lady of Lourdes, glorious in your assumption, triumphant in your coronation, show us the mercy of the Mother of God, Virgin Mary, Queen and Mother, be our comfort, hope, strength and consolation. Amen.

Our Lady of Lourdes, pray for us.
St. Bernadette, pray for us.

Day Four

O Immaculate Queen of heaven, we your children join our prayers of praise and thanksgiving to those of the angels and saints, so that the one, holy Trinity may be glorified in heaven and on earth. Our Lady of Lourdes, as you looked down with love and mercy upon Bernadette as she prayed her rosary in the grotto, look down now, we ask you, with love and mercy upon us. From the abundance of grace granted by your divine Son, give to each of us all that we need, and at this moment look with favor upon the request we seek in this novena (*mention your request here*).

O brilliant star of purity, Mary Immaculate, Our Lady of Lourdes, glorious in your assumption, triumphant in your coronation, show us the mercy of the Mother of God, Virgin Mary, Queen and Mother, be our comfort, hope, strength and consolation. Amen.

Our Lady of Lourdes, pray for us.
St. Bernadette, pray for us.

Day Five

O Mary Immaculate, Mother of God and our mother, from the heights of your dignity look down upon us with mercy while we, full of confidence in your unbounded goodness and confident that your Son will look favorably upon our request, ask you to come to our aid and grant us the favor we seek in this novena (*mention your request here*).

O brilliant star of purity, Mary Immaculate, Our Lady of Lourdes, glorious in your assumption, triumphant in your coronation, show us the mercy of the Mother of God, Virgin Mary, Queen and Mother, be our comfort, hope, strength and consolation. Amen.

Our Lady of Lourdes, pray for us.
St. Bernadette, pray for us.

Day Six

O glorious Mother of God, so wonderful under your special title of Our Lady of Lourdes, to you we raise our hearts and hands to seek your powerful intercession in obtaining from the gracious Heart of Jesus all the help necessary for our spiritual and temporal wellbeing, and for the special favor we so earnestly seek in this novena (mention your request here).

Our Lady of Lourdes, look with compassion upon us today as you did so long ago on Bernadette in the Grotto of Lourdes.

O brilliant star of purity, Mary Immaculate, Our Lady of Lourdes, glorious in your assumption, triumphant in your coronation, show us the mercy of the Mother of God, Virgin Mary, Queen and Mother, be our comfort, hope, strength and consolation. Amen.

Our Lady of Lourdes, pray for us.
St. Bernadette, pray for us.

Day Seven

O Almighty God, who by the Immaculate Conception of the Blessed Virgin Mary did prepare a worthy dwelling place for your Son, we humbly ask that as we contemplate the apparition of Our Lady in the Grotto of Lourdes, we may be blessed with health of mind and body. O most gracious Mother Mary, beloved

Mother of Our Lord and Redeemer, look with favor upon us as you did that day on Bernadette and intercede with him that the favor we now earnestly seek may be granted to us (*mention your request here*).

O brilliant star of purity, Mary Immaculate, Our Lady of Lourdes, glorious in your assumption, triumphant in your coronation, show us the mercy of the Mother of God, Virgin Mary, Queen and Mother, be our comfort, hope, strength and consolation. Amen.

Our Lady of Lourdes, pray for us.
St. Bernadette, pray for us.

Day Eight

O Immaculate Mother of God, from heaven itself you came to appear to young Bernadette in the Grotto of Lourdes. And as Bernadette knelt at your feet and the spring burst forth, and as multitudes have knelt ever since before your shrine, O Mother of God, we kneel before you today to ask that in your mercy you ask your divine Son to grant the special favor we seek in this novena (*mention your request here*).

O brilliant star of purity, Mary Immaculate, Our Lady of Lourdes, glorious in your assumption, triumphant in your coronation, show us the mercy of the Mother of God, Virgin Mary, Queen and Mother, be our comfort, hope, strength and consolation. Amen.

Our Lady of Lourdes, pray for us.
St. Bernadette, pray for us.

Day Nine

O glorious Mother of God, to you we raise our hearts and hands to seek your powerful intercession in obtaining from the loving Heart of Jesus all the graces necessary for our spiritual and temporal wellbeing. O Mother of our divine Lord, as we conclude this novena we ask once again for the special favor we seek in this novena (*mention your request here*).

We are alive with confidence that your prayers on our behalf will be heard. O Mother of my Lord, through the love you bear to Jesus Christ and for the glory of his name, hear our prayers and grant our petitions.

O brilliant star of purity, Mary Immaculate, Our Lady of Lourdes, glorious in your assumption, triumphant in your coronation, show us the mercy of the Mother of God, Virgin Mary, Queen and Mother, be our comfort, hope, strength and consolation. Amen.

Our Lady of Lourdes, pray for us.
St. Bernadette, pray for us.

Prayer to Bernadette

St. Bernadette, little shepherdess of Lourdes, favored with eighteen apparitions of the Immaculate Virgin Mary and with the privilege of lovingly conversing with her, now that you are eternally enjoying the beauty of the Immaculate Mother of God, do not forsake me, your devoted brother (sister) in faith. Intercede for me that I, too, may walk in the simple path of faith. Help me to imitate your example, at our heavenly Mother's request, by praying the rosary daily and by acts of self-denial.

Teach me to imitate your wonderful devotion to God and Our Lady, the Immaculate Conception, so that, like you, I may be blessed with the grace of lasting faithfulness and enjoy the happiness of the eternal vision of God the Father, Son and Holy Spirit. Amen.

God of infinite mercy, we celebrate the feast of Mary, Our Lady of Lourdes, the Mother of God. May her prayers help us to rise above our human weakness. We ask this through our Lord Jesus Christ, your Son, who lives and reigns with you and the Holy Spirit, one God forever. Amen.

O Virgin Immaculate
(Prayer of St. Ephraem of Edessa)

O Virgin Immaculate, Mother of God and my mother, from your sublime heights turn your eyes of pity on me. Filled with confidence in your goodness and knowing full well your power, I beg you to extend to me your assistance in the journey of life, which is so full of dangers for my soul. In order that I may never be a slave of the devil through sin, but may ever live with my heart humble and pure, I entrust myself wholly to you. I consecrate my heart to you forever, my only desire being to love your divine Son, Jesus. Mary, none of your devout servants has ever perished; may I, too, be saved. Amen.

Consecration to Mary

O Mary, Virgin most powerful and mother of mercy, queen of heaven and refuge of sinners, we consecrate ourselves to your immaculate heart.

We consecrate to you our very being and our whole life; all that we have, all that we love, all that we are. To you we give our bodies, our hearts and our souls; to you we give our homes, our families, our country. We desire that all that is in us and around us may belong to you, and may share in the benefits of your motherly blessings. And that this act of consecration may be truly efficacious and lasting, we renew this day the promises of our Baptism and our first Eucharist. We pledge ourselves to profess courageously and at all times the truths of our holy faith, and to live as befits Catholics who are obedient to the Pope and the bishops in communion with him. We pledge ourselves to keep the commandments of God and his Church, in particular to keep holy the Lord's day. We likewise pledge ourselves to make the practices of the Christian religion, and above all the Holy Eucharist, an integral part of our lives.

Finally, we promise you, O glorious Mother of God and loving mother of all humankind, to devote ourselves wholeheartedly to the service of the Kingdom of your Son, so that his Kingdom may come in our own hearts and in those of all people, in our country and in all the world. Amen.

Memorare

Remember, O most gracious Virgin Mary,
that never was it known
that anyone who fled to your protection,
implored your help or sought your intercession,
was left unaided.

Inspired with this confidence
I fly unto you,
O Virgin of virgins, my Mother;
to you do I come,
before you I stand,
sinful and sorrowful;
O Mother of the Word Incarnate,
despise not my petitions,
but in your mercy hear and answer me.
Amen.

Prayer to the Blessed Mother

*W*e fly to your protection, most holy Mother of God; please listen to our petitions and needs, and deliver us from all dangers, ever glorious and blessed Virgin Mary.

Mary, our model and mother, by your obedience and patience you have taught us how to be true children of God. Please help us by your powerful assistance to overcome our weaknesses, and to fulfill well our tasks in life.

By your compassionate aid may we ever stand in spirit with you beneath the cross of Christ so that we may also rejoice with you in your divine Son's triumphant victory over sin and death.

In your maternal kindness help us to be faithful to prayer in the company of God's Church as you were one with the Apostles in the upper room as you waited for the promised Spirit of Pentecost.

With your gracious assistance may we be near you in the glory of Christ's kingdom to sing with you and all the faithful the eternal praise of God. Amen.

O Mary, conceived without sin.
Pray for us who have recourse to you.

You are all fair, O Virgin Mary,
You never knew the stain of sin;
You are the glory of Jerusalem,
You, the joy of Israel,
You, the great honor of our people,
You, the advocate of sinners.
O Mary, Virgin most prudent,
O Mary, Mother most merciful,
Pray for us,
Intercede for us with our Lord,
Jesus Christ.

Litany of Our Lady of Lourdes

Lord have mercy.
Christ have mercy.
Lord have mercy.
Christ hear us.
Christ graciously hear us.

God the Father of heaven, have mercy on us.
God the Son, Redeemer of the world,
    have mercy on us.
God the Holy Spirit, have mercy on us.
Holy Trinity, one God, have mercy on us.

Holy Mary, pray for us.
Holy Mother of God, pray for us.
Mother of Christ, pray for us.
Mother of our Savior, pray for us.

Our Lady of Lourdes, help of Christians,
    pray for us.
Our Lady of Lourdes, source of love,
    pray for us.
Our Lady of Lourdes, mother of the poor,
    pray for us.
Our Lady of Lourdes, mother of the disabled,

pray for us.
Our Lady of Lourdes, mother of orphans,
    pray for us.
Our Lady of Lourdes, mother of all children,
    pray for us.
Our Lady of Lourdes, mother of all nations,
    pray for us.
Our Lady of Lourdes, mother of the Church,
    pray for us.
Our Lady of Lourdes, friend of the lonely,
    pray for us.
Our Lady of Lourdes, comforter of those
    who mourn, pray for us.
Our Lady of Lourdes, shelter of the homeless,
    pray for us.
Our Lady of Lourdes, guide of travelers,
    pray for us.
Our Lady of Lourdes, strength of the weak,
    pray for us.
Our Lady of Lourdes, refuge of sinners,
    pray for us.
Our Lady of Lourdes, comforter of the
    suffering,
        pray for us.
Our Lady of Lourdes, help of the dying,
    pray for us.

Queen of heaven, pray for us.
Queen of peace, pray for us.

Lamb of God,
      you take away the sins of the world,
            spare us O Lord.
Lamb of God,
      you take away the sins of the world,
            graciously hear us, O Lord.
Lamb of God,
      you take away the sins of the world,
            have mercy on us.
Christ hear us. Christ graciously hear us.

Let us pray: Grant us, your servants, we pray you, Lord God, to enjoy health of mind and body. By the glorious intercession of Blessed Mary ever Virgin, may we be delivered from present sorrows, and enjoy everlasting happiness. Through Christ our Lord. Amen.

Lourdes Hymn - "Immaculate Mary"

*I*mmaculate Mary, your praises we sing;
You reign now in splendor
    with Jesus our King.

Ave, ave, ave Maria.
Ave, ave Maria.

In heaven the blessed your glory proclaim;
On earth we your children
    invoke your sweet name.

Ave, ave, ave Maria.
Ave, ave Maria.

Your name is our power,
    your virtues our light,
Your love is our comfort,
    your pleading our might.

Ave, ave, ave Maria.
Ave, ave Maria.

We pray for our mother,
    the Church here on earth;

And bless, holy Mary, the land of our birth.

Ave, ave, ave Maria.
Ave, ave Maria.

Prayer at the Lourdes Grotto in the Vatican Gardens

O blessed Virgin, Mother of God, Mother of Christ, Mother of the Church, look upon us mercifully at this hour. Virgin faithful, pray for us. Teach us to believe as you believed. Make our faith in God, in Christ, in the Church, always to be serene, courageous, strong and generous. Mother worthy of love, Mother of faithful love, pray for us. Teach us to love God and our brothers and sisters as you loved them. Make our love for others to be always patient, kindly and respectful. Cause of our joy, pray for us. Teach us to be able to grasp, in faith, the paradox of Christian joy, which springs up and blooms from sorrow, renunciation, and union with your sacrificed Son. Make our joy to be always genuine and full, in order to be able to communicate it to all. Amen.

The Marian Prayer of Pope John Paul II

Mother of the Redeemer,
with great joy we call you blessed.

In order to carry out his plan of salvation,
God the Father chose you before the creation
    of the world.
You believed in his love and obeyed his word.

The Son of God desired you for his Mother
when he became man to save the human race.
You received him with ready obedience
    and undivided heart.

The Holy Spirit loved you
    as his mystical spouse
and filled you with singular gifts.
You allowed yourself to be led
by his hidden powerful action.

On the eve of the third Christian Millennium,
we entrust to you the Church
which acknowledges you
    and invokes you as Mother.

To you, Mother of the human family
and of the nations,
we confidently entrust the whole of humanity,
with its hopes and fears.
Do not let it lack the light of true wisdom.
Guide its steps in the ways of peace.
Enable all to meet Christ,
The Way, the Truth, and the Life.

Sustain us, O Virgin Mary,
on our journey of faith
and obtain for us the grace of eternal salvation.

O clement, O loving, O sweet Mother of God
and our Mother, Mary!